You Can Do This

Sports Officiating 101

Presented by Referee Lady

Cindy C-Wilson

Table of Contents

Thanks Dad!

Introduction

"Thanks Referee Lady" said the 7th grade football player as I handed him the football in preparation for kick-off. We both smiled, relieving the awkwardness of the moment. This was my first game as a football official and it was his first game with a female referee.

Why did I do this? It was a bit of a dare. After being elected President of the Washington Officials Association, I called my father, who had been officiating football and basketball for 40+ years. I told him my idea. I said something about how cool it would be to officiate a football or volleyball game with him. His fatherly and professionally honest response was "Yes, that would be great, but it probably won't happen." Knowing he would not learn how to referee volleyball, I started down the path of learning to referee high school football. This opportunity was made possible by the efforts of many people. Finally, on a beautiful fall day in October, the game took place. The field was behind the junior high I had attended many years ago. My old school team was playing a rival opponent from the neighboring city.

I was assigned as the Linesman, which added a fourth position to a normally three person crew. That didn't matter. We all knew working with my dad was as important to me as doing my best for the athletes. The Referee was a 50+ year veteran official and had actually taught both head coaches at one time or another in his middle school classroom. My dad was the Umpire. The Field Judge, also a veteran of many decades, rounded out the crew. Was it overkill for a seventh grade football game? Probably. They were doing it partially for me but mostly out of their devotion to the sport and the kids. Did the players know they had a female official? After a while they did. And the parents indicated they thought it was pretty cool. As for making news, the local paper ran a very nice article about the event as did Referee Magazine, February 2008.

To this day, my appreciation for this opportunity runs very deep and is a highlight of my officiating career. This is how Referee Lady came about and I hope you find the information useful as well as entertaining.

Thank you for reading *You Can Do This: Sports Officiating 101.*

Chapter One: Why Officiate?

The question is "Why Officiate?" As a prospective or current official, your answer to this question is your key. It belongs to you and only you. The answer may change over time. Understanding why you do this or why you would want to do this is important. Remembering your 'Why?' will help move you through the sometimes tough preparation. It will also get you through those games that seem to go on indefinitely. In reality, they do end at some point.

The answers to the question of 'Why?' come from many different experiences and events. It could be that you enjoyed playing the sport in your younger years and want to give back. That is a great start. There were officials at your games. Even if you do not remember them, they had to be there or you would not have been able to play. Perhaps you were unable to play for one reason or another and now find yourself in a position to participate.

If the answer to your 'Why?' is because you think you are going to get rich officiating, then perhaps you should re-think that answer. Refereeing to earn extra money is an answer, but a good official keeps in mind that it is not about the paycheck. Yes, you may get paid to officiate the game, but the financial reward falls way short of the intangible rewards that come from officiating.

Perhaps your answer to this question pops into mind while watching your own children play. You learned a lot while watching countless hours of practice and games while they participated in a sport. Certainly you could do as well as that official, or maybe you would not have missed that particular foul? If you sit through enough games, you get a feel for what should be happening, even if you do not agree. This is an important impetus for you to get involved. Once you go through the training and officiate some games of your own, watching your children play takes on a whole new perspective. You often gain a new respect for the officials you watch.

Whatever your answer is to 'Why Officiate?' keep that in mind during preparation, during the game(s) and again during feedback. A strong, passionate answer will help you stay 'grounded' as well as keep you moving forward.

Chapter Two: Preparation

Preparation is one of the keys to a successful officiating career.   From beginning officials to those who do Super Bowls, World Series or National Championships, each level demands preparation.   There are multiple phases to preparation and each one requires attention.

Physical

Officiating sports demands some level of fitness. Making sure you can get up and down the court, field, pitch, diamond or rink with the players is the measure of your fitness.   Even if your sport of choice does not mean running and keeping up with the athletes, presentation of professionalism and confidence shows the athletes and coaches that you are taking care of yourself. It shows that you deserve to be there because you have physically prepared for the game. This does not mean you must bench press 400 pounds or run a sub-4 minute mile. It means you are prepared for the level of fitness demanded by your chosen sport. If you officiate sports year round, then doing something in addition to your game time is important to make sure you have a solid fitness baseline. Part of making sure you are fit is eating right and getting enough sleep. Many of us hurry from our 9-5 job to the field without thinking about the fuel our body needs to perform at its peak. While you may be able to go through an evening game 'OK', preparation for these nights is crucial. It is not always necessary to have a full 3 or 4 course meal beforehand, but knowing what your body needs to maintain a high level of performance is important. Listening to what your body is trying to tell you is a great indication of what you should do. Do you just need a bigger than normal lunch on game days and a light snack before the game? Do you need to pack snacks, like granola, energy or protein bars, nuts, sport drinks, water or maybe even a peanut butter and jelly sandwich to eat during intermission or half-time? Keep it simple and know that you can always eat again after the event. Make sure to be properly fueled and hydrated for the duration of the game. Sleep is very important in keeping your body and mind in good health. Make sure you are getting enough rest, not just hours lying in bed, but quality time sleeping.

Rules

Each sport has its own set of rules or multiple sets of rules, depending on the particular level. As an example, you may watch football on Saturday afternoons, Sundays and/or Monday nights; this does not mean that those are the same rules that would be applied on Friday nights. High school rules are different from college and professional rules. High school sports are considered an 'extension of the classroom'. What you think you may know from watching a sport at the college or professional level is different at high school and lower levels. Reading the rulebook for your specific level of officiating is one important key to success. Case books and manuals are also essential tools. These written materials are good beginning guidelines which lead to asking questions and having discussions with those around you that may have more experience. Many state associations offer sports specific rules clinics in which coaches and officials gather pre-season to discuss any rule changes and points of emphasis. This is a great opportunity to be exposed to other points of view. There is always more than one way to see a particular play. More experience does not always mean 'right,' so be sure and take information with a grain of salt and an eye as to how you might have responded in a similar situation. Situational scenario discussions are helpful, as long as they cover the majority of what could happen at the game. Spending copious amounts of time on things that could happen 1% of the time is a waste of energy. Let the 1% happen, deal with it the best you can at the time, then put that in your own collection of experiences. The 1% experiences make some of the best human interest stories. One that comes to mind is the time the high school football player 'told' the umpire he should have given him a 2 minute warning, to which the umpire replied, "I'll give you that 2 minute warning when we play on Sundays." It's all in the delivery.

Mechanics

Signals are how officials 'tell the story' or communicate to those watching and participating in the game. Most rule books have at least a few pages of illustrations of what mechanics or signals should look like. Be proud and confident of your signals. Make your signals big and clear. If you are unsure of the mechanic or signal, ask someone to help you out. Mechanics may differ from rule book to rule book so be sure you are giving the correct signals. Apply high school mechanics at a high school game and not college mechanics that you may have been practicing for a college game. Practice your signals in a mirror and or video tape for immediate feedback. Looking confident and sharp will increase your credibility and your ability to 'sell' the call.

Mentor

Find a mentor, or two. Learn and practice your craft and then be a mentor to others. Use mentors to talk through situations not specified in a rule book or case book. Every game offers an opportunity for something new to occur and add to your experience. You may already have a mentor, which is why you are interested in pursuing officiating as an avocation or vocation. Good mentors are golden. Those with experience, patience and a willingness to help you be successful are priceless. Learn from them and make sure that when it is your turn to mentor you are golden. Golden mentors can make your experience and growth positive, memorable and fun. If you have a less than positive mentor and want to continue learning, tell someone who can do something about it. The last thing a newer official needs is someone telling them the wrong things to do, blasting them when they make a mistake, and focusing the relationship on the mentor and how "cool" they are. Learning how not to be a golden mentor can be as important as learning how to be golden. Be golden!

Being prepared in all aspects of officiating includes being a student of the game. Knowing how the game is played and coached allows you to understand and appreciate the role you play as the official. Everyone has a role and we need to make sure we are prepared to do our best.

Chapter Three: Execution

I have a friend who has a different spin on the cliché, 'Practice makes perfect' which goes, 'Practice makes toward perfection.' The latter is a more accurate version of the cliché with regard to officiating and it does not matter what sport.

Practice

What does 'practice' look like? Find a team at a nearby school at the beginning of the season and talk with the coach. Ask if s/he would mind if you came to some of their workouts to practice blowing your officiating whistle. I am not aware of any coach that would not like to be able to simulate game time during part of practice. Not only are you practicing, but many of these young athletes have not played in the presence of an official. The only whistle they may be used to is the one their coach uses during practice, not an officials' whistle ending the play. Thus, everyone is learning at the same time. This kind of reaching out and collaborating is priceless. Another practice option is using pre-season, non-league, mini-games or jamborees. These can involve multiple teams in a short period of time and are a great opportunity to get instant feedback. Practicing the adjustments right away helps in preparation for the upcoming season. Going this extra step shows the athletes and coaches that officials also need to prepare for game day. This can go a long way in putting a human face on those 'striped' referee uniforms. Another option would be to volunteer at the local Boys and Girls Clubs. Not only do you get to practice your skills, but you will be giving back to the community at the same time.

Game Time

Game time preparation is as complete as possible. You are fit, know the rules, have practiced your signals and are well rested. You have communicated with your partner(s) about expectations. Now it is time to put on your game face. Know you have done your best to understand and prepare for what it takes to officiate the game. Even with full planning, things are not always black and white when you get on the field, court, diamond, pitch or rink. All you can do is give your best effort. You are human. It is okay to make a mistake. You must own it and then fix it. You will increase your credibility. Look professional, be confident and approachable. Have fun!!! Life is too short to do something you do not enjoy.

Chapter Four: Evaluation

What Worked Well

Preparation paid off. You knew the rules and when to apply them. You looked and felt confident. You were early enough to have time to discuss expectations with your partner(s) before the game. You and your partner(s) made time after the game to debrief. You learned something new, were part of the team and are looking forward to the next assignment.

What Could Be Done Better

More preparation may be needed for next time. Maybe your whistle wasn't loud enough or you were unsure of the proper signal. Perhaps a situation arose and you realized more time was needed to discuss it with your partner(s). Whatever happened, use it as a learning experience to be built on, practiced and remembered for future games. Be sure to be open and welcome feedback from other officials in your crew. If applicable, share your experience with others to help them with their preparation. Take one experience at a time. Trying to capture them all at one time could be overwhelming and ending in none of them being addressed. Do the best you can, learn from the experience, and continue to grow and share.

Chapter Five: Ladies Only

Ladies, this chapter is for you. If you are thinking 'I can't do that', then please, think again.

Many of you have participated in some level of sports, even at the college level. Since Title IX was implemented in the late 1970's more females have had the opportunity to play than ever before; with about a 560% increase at the college level and over 900% at the high school level *(Women's Sports Foundation, March 2013).* This is not a political stance or viewpoint, just a statement of fact. It is up to you to give back to the sport(s) that allowed you to experience teamwork, gain success through preparation and enable you to be the person you are today.

Even if you did not participate in sports, officiating is something you can do! This is something both men and women can do. Even though it has been mostly men up to this point, women can and are making a difference. At the high school and middle school levels, it is not so much about "Who is wearing the stripes?" as it is about "Is there someone in stripes on the field so we can play?"

The 'glass ceiling' in officiating is really just 'a thick layer of men'. Women have the same ability to learn, practice and become proficient at officiating all sports. We just have to believe we have what it takes to get there, stay there and mentor those coming behind us. There are still men who resist this entrance into the officiating world and can make it difficult. Women need to be strong and let them know we are here to work together *with* them, not against them.

Yes, we do have additional 'challenges'. We are the ones who have the children, which can cut into our practice and game times. We also have the additional issues about uniforms that do not always fit right off the rack, especially for those sports not currently flush with female officials (football and baseball come to mind). And, even if the uniforms do fit, we often have to take extra pre-cautions to make sure our 'girls' are properly supported, more for our own health than for the obvious viewing of the fans. These are just a couple of issues faced by women as we start down the officiating road. None of which are insurmountable, they just make our answer to 'Why' and our resolve to succeed that much stronger.

Today it is easier to begin and continue to officiate. The women who came before and persevered have paved the way. Uniforms are starting to be designed for women so that is becoming less of a challenge. Female officials are becoming more and more accepted by coaches, players and fans and less a novelty. One of the changes helping with this acceptance is that more and more women are also coaching. The path is clearing for those of us interested in continuing our sports passion.

This is an exciting time for women in sports. As higher and higher levels of participation open up, we need to be ready to step up and meet that opportunity head on, prepared and confident.

Chapter Six: You Can Do This

None of us can do this alone. We have to have partners during preparation and on the field, court, pitch, rink or diamond.   We need support from friends and family. Although they may not understand why we do this, we need them by our side and 'in our corner'. Find or build a support network to help. Whether it is someone with a sympathetic ear to listen to your post-game review, helps watch the kids while you go officiate, gives you feedback while practicing your signals or makes sure your uniform fits. Support is critical to success.

Often our friends and family do not understand why we do this because we don't tell them. We do not tend to share our 'Why' with them so, of course, how would they know? It is up to us to share our 'Why' and our experiences, good or bad, so they can attempt to understand. They do not have to pick up the rule book and learn to officiate; we really just want them to give us room to do that ourselves. We want them to try and appreciate why we lace up every Friday night to go get muddy on the football field or pitch. Why having a clean and pressed uniform is important to us, even though in about an hour it may be drenched with sweat from running up and down the court or the field.

Perhaps no one but other officials can truly understand why we do this, and even they may not realize what drives each one of us. They just know that it is important to do.

If it is important enough to do, it is important enough to make sure you do it well. Preparation and realistic expectations go far in providing a positive experience. Everything we do in life starts with that first step and moves forward one step at a time. Just as athletes learn the game and gain experience, so do we as officials. So allow yourself the patience and respect you deserve when you begin this journey. Do not be too hard on yourself. When a mistake is made, and mistakes will be made, use it as feedback to apply next time during preparation or a game. Share your experiences with others. Enjoy the teamwork necessary to prepare for and conduct the game. Include your friends and family in the experience and by all means – enjoy what you are doing!

Although some of this information may seem daunting, it is good to put it into perspective. We do this because of our answer to the question at the beginning of this book "Why Officiate?" This is only a part of our life, not the whole of who and what we are. Officiating sports enhances that part of us that may not be expressed in any other opportunity or avenue. This gives us the chance to interact with student athletes and make a difference. We build memories and life experiences only available to those who step out of their comfort zone. That comfort zone expands in ways we may not understand or foresee, but each experience makes our lives fuller and richer.

Whether you are male or female, young or old, thinking about starting or already experienced in officiating, you can do this. Because, after all the preparation, practice, feedback and experience, it is about having your very own 'Thanks Referee Lady' moment.

You Can Do This!